THE GREAT BOOK OF ANIMAL KNOWLEDGE

GORILLAS

Strongest of the Great Apes

Introduction

Gorillas are closely related to humans and are very intelligent. The big, plant-eating, tree-swinging gorillas are very few and are only found in Africa. Poachers and habitat loss are the gorilla's biggest threats today. Gorillas are one of the most interesting animals.

What Gorillas Look Like

Gorillas' stomachs are wider than their chests. Their arms are longer than their legs, giving them a rather upright position when they walk on all fours. They also have a bulging forehead. All gorillas have black or brown-grey hair, but grown up male gorillas will grow silver-gray hair on their backs and on their upper legs. Gorillas grow more hair on their upper and lower bodies, leaving the middle part of their body with short hair. Their chests also have short hair.

Size and Weight

The gorilla is the largest of the apes, which include chimpanzees and bonobos. The male gorillas are much larger than the female gorillas, weighing about 400 pounds with a height of 6 feet, while females weigh 250 pounds and are 5 feet tall.

Senses

The senses of a gorilla are almost like those of humans. And just like humans, all these senses serve an important part in their life. They hear to locate one another and detect approaching danger, they see to find and identify their food as well as for looking out for danger, and they smell for different odors in the air that tell them different things.

Grooming

Grooming is an important activity in the gorillas' life. Gorillas groom each other to improve bonding time together and strengthen relationships within their family. Grooming usually includes getting mites out of their fur and eating it, or combing each other with their fingers. Only the male leader in a group does not groom.

Strength

Gorillas are very strong animals. The strongest part of their body is their arms because it is the most used part. They use it for swinging from branch to branch. It's also used for walking, and getting food. Adult males, called silverbacks, are the strongest gorillas. They can pick up heavy objects and throw them with ease.

Intelligence

Gorillas are very smart animals. They can communicate with humans through sign language. They can spot snares ahead of them, and even know how to destroy the snare. A gorilla was seen checking how deep a pond was with a tree branch. They can even express their feelings like us humans. Scientists experimented if a gorilla would recognize themselves through a mirror, and some gorillas were able to.

Where Gorillas Live

Gorillas are mostly found in Western Africa. They live in tropical forests. Most gorillas live in the lowland forests, while others stay in the highest parts of the mountains. Gorillas actually prefer staying on the ground than on treetops. They will most likely climb a tree to get the foods they need.

What Gorillas Do

Gorillas spend most of their time eating, going around, and resting. This resting period is usually when they socialize with each other, either by grooming each other or playing with each other.

Where Gorillas Sleep

Gorillas never sleep in the same spot as where they slept before. They build a new nest every time they are going to sleep, even if it's just a few feet away from their old nest. Every gorilla in a group makes their own nests; mothers make for themselves and their babies. Female and young male gorillas tend to make their nests on trees, while the silverback, leader of the group, hardly ever makes his nest on a tree. The nest is made out of plants and bushes, or branches if they're up a tree, tied together.

What Gorillas Eat

Even though gorillas are herbivores – plant-eaters—they will sometimes eat small animals (mostly insects), like termites and caterpillars. However, they mostly eat a variety of plants and fruits. They climb trees to get to the fruits. And they also, though not usually, eat soil because of the minerals they need that's lacking from their plant diet.

Drinking

Gorillas don't usually drink water because the plants they eat are succulent, meaning they contain a lot of water in them. But if they come across a river, they use the hair at the back of their hands to absorb the water so that they can suck it when they are feeling thirsty.

Troops

Gorillas live in a group called a troop. A troop contains a male leader, called a silverback. The silverback is the most important member of the troop. He is the one who decides when they move out, resolves conflicts within the troop, and is the one who fights when the troop is under attack. The rest of the troop is taken by females and their babies. Other adult males in a group are not really part of the troop, but they are allowed to live with them until they can find their own troop. There can also be a leading female, but she is not powerful compared to the silverback. Gorillas in a troop are very close to each other.

Territory

Gorillas are not territorial, meaning they don't stick to one area of land and guard it from intruders. In fact, gorillas roam around in different land areas every day. When a troop meets another troop, the two silverbacks of each troop will engage in a fight, the winner will claim the dead silverback's troop. Sometimes, however, when troops meet they just ignore each other.

Communication

The most common communication for the gorilla is the beating of their chests. The beating of the chest is usually connected to a fight. The silverback will stand upright and beat his chests rapidly with his hands while making a screaming sound. But they also have other ways to communicate, either by sound or without sound. They can growl, grunt, and even hoot like an owl. They can also laugh and stick their tongues out to make fun of others.

Breeding

For gorillas, mating seasons are year-round, meaning they can mate anytime of the year. Female gorillas become mature at seven or eight years old, but don't breed until a few years later. Male gorillas mature even longer, about 15 years old. A female gorilla will be pregnant for 8 months, and will usually give birth to just one infant.

Baby Gorillas

Baby gorillas are called infants. An infant will be nursed, cared for, and taught by their mother and other members of the troop for at least 4 years. Even a silverback takes care of the infants. Mother gorillas are very protective of their young, and will fight other gorillas who want to kill them. Infants can start walking at 8 months old, but before that, they ride on their mother's back. When the male infants reach 11 years old, they will leave their troop to make their own troop.

Predators

Gorillas don't really have enemies. The only predator for the gorilla is a leopard. When a leopard attacks, the silverback will stand in front of the leopard, while the female gorillas will group together and stay at the back of the silverback. The silverback protects his troop members from the leopard. Infants are very in danger from leopards if they go far away from the troops.

Endangered

Gorillas are now endangered, meaning there are only a few of them left. A female gorilla can give birth to only 4 infants in her lifetime. Slow reproduction rates, and the fact that poachers – people who kill gorillas -- are killing them at a speedy rate, are the main reasons why gorillas are now endangered. Habitat destruction is also another reason why they are now endangered. Many of the forests they live in are being cut down.

Mountain Gorillas

Mountain gorillas are the gorillas that live in the mountains. They have thicker fur than the other gorillas to protect them from the cold. Their arms are also shorter than the lowland gorillas. Mountain gorillas are the largest kinds of gorillas.

Lowland Gorillas

Photo by Herman Pijpers (flickr.com/8259447@N06), as licensed under CC BY 2.0 Generic

Lowland gorillas live in the lowlands. They are much more likely to be seen on trees. They live in a more forest-like, flat area compared to the home of the mountain gorillas. Lowland gorillas tend to eat more fruits than plants.

Get the next book in this series!

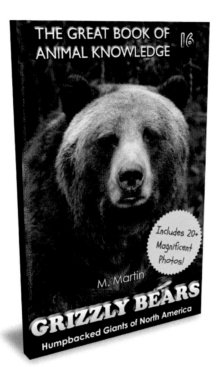

GRIZZLY BEARS: Humpbacked Giants of North America

Log on to Facebook.com/GazelleCB for more info

Tip: Use the key-phrase "The Great Book of Animal Knowledge" when searching for books in this series.

For more information about our books, discounts and updates, please Like us on Facebook!

Facebook.com/GazelleCB

Made in the USA
Coppell, TX
27 May 2021